To:
Millie
Purpose us
Prosperity!.

Stay In Your Lane

Know Yourself. Love Yourself. Live On Purpose.

Stay In Your Lane

Know Yourself. Love Yourself. Live On Purpose.

Kamryn Adams

IMPRESA
BOOKS

Published by Impresa Books

Impresa Books
The Kamryn Adams Group LLC
New Brunswick, New Jersey

10 9 8 7 6 5 4 3 2 1

ISBN:9-780-990871309 (Paperback)
Printed in The United States of America

"Just find out what you have that works and work it!"

Kamryn Adams

I'd like to extend my deepest gratitude to the following ladies for your contribution to this project:

Mikeisha Anderson
Simone Anderson
Mikeila Bowen
Marie Dukes
Avis Goode
Nicole Pertillar
Denna Singleton

To the ladies of the 2014 IAY Conference:
Thank you for a warm welcome and supporting my work.

1 Timothy 1:14

-1-
"I think the reward for conformity is that everyone likes you except yourself."
– Rita Mae Brown

If you're happy and you know it clap your hands. Clap! Clap! If you're pretty and you know it clap your hands! Silence. If you're smart and you know it clap your hands! Silence. If you're great and you know it and you really want to show it, if you're fabulous and you know it clap your hands. Silence again.

People are afraid to clap for themselves. It is not because you do not think you are pretty. Nor is it because you do not think that you are smart. It is because you have been taught to downplay all the wonderful things about yourself in the spirit of being humble. But that misconstrued messaging of "being humble" has evolved into a society of people who have no idea what value they bring to the world.

If you look up "humble" in the dictionary there are several definitions. As an adjective, humble can mean having a feeling of insignificance or inferiority as in "I came from humble beginnings." Being humble can also mean being courteously respectful as in "In my humble opinion…"

However, the top definition for humble is "not proud or arrogant." This is the definition that has been lost in translation over time. Being humble does not mean that you shrink yourself and your gifts. It means that you are not so taken by your own greatness that you refuse to acknowledge or value the greatness of others.

Our gifts, talents, and greatness are not with respect to those around us. They are simply traits that God has given us to fulfill a purpose in the world. If we never acknowledge that greatness, we never achieve our purpose. Chances are, you are not happy with yourself if you are not living your life on purpose. If you are not happy with yourself it is impossible to be genuinely happy for anyone around you. Impossible!

Referencing the song in the first paragraph, we often know "it" but we do not want people to know we know it. Why? Insecurity. Fear. Laziness. Apathy. These are all reasons that we do not clap for ourselves. True humility is rarely the reason we lack applause for ourselves.

I know it is warm and cozy hiding underneath the covers. But, the longer we stay curled up refusing to look in the mirror the more we forget what we look like and who we really are. Once you forget who you are, you are in danger of being defined by the world around you. You become a product of the people and problems in your life.

Over the years, I have run into so many people who were tossed around by what society and circumstance told them they were supposed to be. Our parents, our neighborhoods, our education, our financial situation, and even our birth order all send silent messages as to who we should be. So you find yourself standing face to face with your reflection and asking, "Mirror, mirror on the wall, who the heck am I?"

As for me, it took years before I truly looked in the mirror and accepted who I was created to be. It is easy for most of us to shine light on our flaws and imperfections. We may not admit it in a public forum, but we can identify every negative thing we feel about ourselves. It is a much more difficult task to lovingly accept and identify with the greatness inside of us.

It was a chore for me to be me. To walk in my gifts, believe in my purpose, and accept my unique ability was a challenge for me. Sometimes it was fear. Other times it was apathy. Most times I was just being plain lazy and taking the easy way through life.

I was smart enough to get a higher education. I was charismatic enough to land a great job. I was driven enough to climb the corporate ladder. It did not take much effort to collect my check each week. Heck, they even deposited it right into my bank account. I woke up every other Friday morning and there it was – my provision.

I got really comfortable in the easy way of life. There was no deeper meaning to ponder. There was no calling that pulled me toward something bigger. I had quite nearly replaced WHO I AM with WHAT I DO.

One day as I was gazing into the mirror and I got a glimpse of someone. I recognized her as someone I knew from years ago, back before conformity and courtesy smothered individuality and authenticity. She was brilliant, talented, pretty, kind, and very capable with a giving heart and fabulous hair. I smiled at her but she did not smile back. It felt great to see her again. Though she clearly did not feel the same way. I took a closer look and I started to panic. I realized that she was a ghost. I killed this young woman long ago and for that reason, she was now being unkind to me.

I had been playing in the shadows for a long time. I denied who I AM for so long that the belief I once held as being intentionally and wonderfully made had morphed into a questionable worry about who I really was and what I was supposed to be doing with my life.

The more I accepted my own greatness the more I started to see more clearly the greatness in others. The more I saw greatness buried in others, the more I realized how often people had strangled that greatness in the comfort of conformity.

So how do we get to our unique brand of greatness? The first step is to know yourself. You have to believe that God created you with a unique set of skills and talents. He created you with destiny and purpose. You need to spend the time and put in the work to figure out what you have that works. Get a coach. Go to counseling. Read some books. Once you know what tools you have, it will be easier to identify which of life's lanes you will journey.

After you get to know yourself, you must learn to love yourself. This step is sometimes the hardest and takes the longest amount of time. We claim to love God with all of our hearts. Yet we do not love and embrace who He has made us to be.

The creator is defined by his or her creation. Think of your favorite musician or artist. You have never heard anyone say, "I love Mary J Blige, but I don't care much for her music." Who says, "Oh I love Picasso but I care nothing for his paintings." You came to "love" the creator because you had a great appreciation and respect for his/her creation.

We do not take this same approach with God, whom we say is our creator. We are brunettes who wish to be blonde. We are dancers who wish to be singers. We are scientists who wish we could draw. We have accepted God in our minds as our creator but have not developed a love and appreciation for his handiwork in our hearts.

Our self-loathing behavior and lack of appreciation for who God has made us can be translated this way: "I love you God, but you really messed up when you made me. You did not know what you were doing."

The creation is always an extension of the creator. Acknowledging that God created you just the way you are is a prerequisite to building a higher self-esteem and more positive self-image. You grew to love God. Now you need to grow to appreciate His marvelous work. The two go hand in hand. You cannot say you love God without loving others. Ironically, it is impossible to love others if you do not first love yourself.

Self-love is the foundation for finding your lane in life. You cannot find your purpose without loving and understanding who you are and all that you have to offer this life. It is not until you appreciate your unique talents that you will understand how best to use them to fulfill your purpose.

The preparatory step to greatness is to live your life on purpose or as you have heard it said, "stay in your lane." You must realize that you were created for a purpose. You did not come into the world simply to put another body on the earth. You were born as your race and gender at a specific time, in a specific place to fulfill a specific purpose in the world. When you realize that you have a purpose, you then start to embrace your story as a necessary part of the journey. Think of the circumstances and events of your life as the pavement that creates your lane.

Once you accept that you were created perfectly and for a purpose, you then begin to love yourself enough to explore the inner workings of "YOU" as a being, not just a body. You start to move beyond wishing you were taller or able to play sports and on to more intimate traits like connection, truth, authenticity, and choice. That exploration is the path to self-love, which manifests in a great love for everyone around you. It creates an intimate love of God, who created you.

Do you know your purpose? My purpose is love. In all that I do my purpose prevails. My mission is to guide others into self-love and be a conduit for God's love in the world. I live my life on "Loving Walk Lane" and I am never moving off my street.

My goal is for everyone I encounter to walk away with a clear understanding of God's love, which leads to self-love and ultimately a love for others. When you love yourself, you no longer need to define who you are in comparison to the people and things around you. When you are in your lane, the situations that befall you do not define you. You will be on your own journey on your own private road.

You will no longer feel the need to pretend to be something other that what you are. Your light will shine so brightly that you will not need to dim the light of others. You will illuminate your lane without giving a single thought to the person in the lane next to you. Life is not a race. Life is a journey that we happen to be taking at the same time as other people born in our era.

Once you love yourself you will find it much easier to love everybody else. I know it sounds crazy, but it is true. You can measure the love you have for yourself by directly assessing the love you have for everyone around you. That includes your children, your mate, your friends, your family, and perfect strangers. If you do not love yourself, it is impossible to love others. Without love, you will never find your purpose.

Your life story is the pavement for the road you will travel. Love fuels the journey that keeps you moving forward. Your purpose is your lane.

Take some time to think about what you want to name your lane. It's okay if you do not know exactly where you want to live right now. Use pencil and keep changing it until you truly discover your lane. If you do not know your lane yet, give it a name that illustrates just that i.e., "Who The Heck Knows Lane."

-2-

"The best and most beautiful things in the world cannot be seen or even touched - they must be felt with the heart." - Helen Keller

Many people start the morning with positive affirmations. We use these encouraging statements to enhance our esteem and give us confidence to move about our day. "You are beautiful. You are beautiful. You are beautiful." We say this over and over again. We put sticky notes on our mirrors and computer screens. These are the kinds of loving things we say to ourselves.

Imagine the beginning of your day. You are well rested and feel confident that everything you touch this day will be a huge success. You have a meeting or gathering among people you do not know. The leader of the group asks you to tell three things about yourself. You say, "I am beautiful. I am amazing. I am special."

How did reading that last paragraph make you feel? Did you laugh? Smile in irony? Roll your eyes? Twist your lips in conforming doubt? If you heard someone else in a meeting say this, how would you feel about that person? We are conditioned to shrink in the presence of others and condemn or judge those who do not choose to join us.

At some point in our lives we each knew that we had something really great about us. We realized we could dance or sing. We realized we were fast runners. We realized we had gifted hands. We realized people were drawn to us. We realized we could remember things other people could not. There was something about us that we knew was our thing. It was our "it".

Then somewhere along the way someone told you to play "it" down. If you were a pretty little girl, you were still a young unassuming girl the first time you heard someone say, "She thinks she's cute."

I remember it well. I was dolled up for my birthday in a new pink and white jumpsuit. My mom had fixed my hair into two pigtails that hung to my shoulders, each wrapped with that fuzzy pink ribbon that used to leave lint on your clothes. I thought I was cute. I felt good about my birthday attire. I felt good that it was my birthday. Then as soon as I arrived in the masses someone said, "Look at you. You think you're cute."

The way she said it let me know that I was not supposed to think I was cute. Other people could think I was cute but I could not. So I shouted with intensity, "No I don't think I'm cute."

And so it began...a lifetime of negative confessions and self-doubt engendered by false humility. The more you say you do not think you are cute, the more you start to believe it. Before long, I started to think I was simply a bit above average –

nothing to write home about but not scaring the animals away.

We often make negative confessions about ourselves and play down our positive traits in order for people to believe that we are "humble" – that word again. On that particular day, I thought I was cute. I did not necessarily think I was prettier than other girls. Actually that was not at all my concern.

It was my birthday and so I was really only thinking about myself and how I looked. I was not thinking about how I looked in comparison to the other preteen girls on the planet. On that day I certainly could have been indicted on being a narcissist. However, I was not arrogant or "conceited" as charged.

Somehow the notion of self-confidence became conceit. The two are not the same. As we wallowed in our own trough of low esteem we became critical of others who seemed to better understand their worth. It made us uncomfortable and so we judged them as conceited.

I came to learn that it was okay for me to think that I was attractive as long as I remembered two things. First, that God created me in this shell for His glory and purpose. Second, my physical appearance in no way defines me. There is very little you can learn about me by looking at me from across the room. My physical appearance is merely the container for who I AM.

Sure, we can acknowledge that society plays some favorites for being cute but that external beauty does absolutely nothing for our wholeness. Whether we are considered plain or perfect, it is important for us not to take our looks too seriously.

It is quite okay for you to acknowledge that you love some of your physical traits. The key is to not get so caught up in the physical that you ignore what is really important: WHO YOU ARE.

Your body is simply a shell that houses you. You should take good care of it and love it, of course. But you must realize that "YOU" live inside of that body. There is no sense getting overly excited about the physical form you have been created with because it will, without a doubt, change and pass away.

We struggle so much with self-image as modern day women and girls. Now, even young men struggle with physical esteem. Are they muscular enough or tall enough or handsome enough?

Airbrush and Photoshop have made it impossible and unrealistic to achieve the images that we aspire to be as we are sweating off the pounds on the treadmills and pounding out chest presses.

Some men and women who are in their forties and fifties are falling into depression over loosing muscle tone or having tiny love handles. They are measuring themselves against external images - ones that have been enhanced by digital and artistic invention. It is much easier to create a digital six-pack than to actually build one in your abdominal core.

If you couple this digitally enhanced imaging with years of being told to diminish your physical beauty, you have a very potent serum of poor self-image and low self-esteem. We have all tasted the bittersweet concoction of self-image sabotage. We look in the mirror and sigh at what we see. We make negative confessions that we are unhappy with the way we look.

With false humility and seeing pictures that remove every wrinkle and flap from the body, it has become more than a challenge to be pleased with the reflection in the mirror. But, you must look closer.

Everyone is struggling to feel good about themselves in the midst of selfies and snap chats. I have seen people take numerous shots to get the perfect selfie. It takes three, four, and five attempts to get a photo that does not show forehead wrinkles. We need to minimize the slight double chin or that one tooth that sits a little crooked on the side of your mouth.

We have gotten so obsessive about our appearance that school pictures now offer to fix your blemishes, whiten your teeth and brush out any imperfections in your portraits. There was a time when having a zit in your tenth grade portrait was an adolescent memory - something to laugh about at high school reunions. Now it is erased from the canvas and our mind. The messaging to our children is toxic.

On one hand, we are hyper obsessed about looking perfect. Yet, when we feel like we look great, we must play it down to continue mastery of our conformity. This behavior is not at all being authentically humble. It is false humility and it leads to low self-awareness that eventually erodes into lower self-esteem.

So, here's what you do…

Teach yourself to love how you look. Find something physical that you love about yourself. Then look in the mirror, take a deep breath and force yourself to admit just how beautiful you are. Keep saying it until you see it. Keep saying it until you really believe it.

We all started out thinking that we were perfectly made. If you cannot remember that time in your life, watch small children in the midst of adults. They strut around knowing they are the center of the universe. They own the love of everyone around them.

Everything they do requires applause and cheers…crawling, walking, going to the potty. We build up the esteem of our children and then the world slowly erodes it in the name of "humility" and sometimes we help with that task.

You have to blot out all the negative messages and unrealistic images that have been planted inside of you over the years. Allow yourself to love the way you look and the way you do things. Give yourself permission to love the way you are.

It helps to acknowledge that you were created by God, wonderfully and fearfully made I might add. I like to look in the mirror and just bask in the great job God did with my shell. Yep, sometimes I look in the mirror and say, "Wow! Thank you Lord. You did an amazing job with me."

When I look in the mirror, I can totally see that one of my eyes is bigger than the other and it sometimes makes me look cross-eyed in photographs. My birthmark sits on the tip of my nose. For my whole life, people have come to me and told me that I had a smudge on my nose. My feet are not symmetrical and my neck is long and striated.

I am not physically flawless. But I do believe that I am flawlessly created to be just me. I am the best looking me there is on the planet. That is simply amazing. That is simply the foundational truth of physical beauty.

After you have become self-aware and begin to appreciate your physical attributes and personal image, you then need to keep yourself in check from comparing yourself to other people. Many times we can only like ourselves in the face of someone that we feel is inferior to us. Therefore your self-image fluctuates and you never truly develop an individual esteem around your self-image.

For example, if you are a size 8, you feel amazing when you are around women who are size 12 and 14 but you shrink in inadequacy when you are around women who are size 2 and 4. Ridiculous!!! If you are happy being a size 8, you should not be happier around people bigger than you or disappointed around people smaller than you. You simply need to focus on whether or not you feel good about YOU, irrespective of anybody else in the world.

When you acknowledge that you are perfectly created in physical form your self-image will not fluctuate based upon who is around you. You will be able to develop a healthy respect for your physical traits without putting an overemphasis on external factors that have very little to do with who you are. This notion is important to teach young people the value of physical appearance and personal care while not neglecting the emotional, mental and spiritual components which is actually who you are.

Sometimes when I do a workshop on building self-image I start out with a table full of gifts. I have big boxes and little boxes. I have them wrapped up in different papers. Some packages are big and shiny and others are small and tattered with a variety in between.

I play a game with the participants (usually young girls) and let them compete for prizes. Each girl can pick the box when she answers correctly. We hold the boxes at our tables and then we open them all at once. The girls find that the biggest shiniest box (usually picked first) is empty. The small brown box with no wrapping paper (always gets picked last) has a twenty-dollar bill in it. The young lady who choses the tattered box can keep the money for herself.

Silence falls across the room and the light bulb comes on for the girls. Though our physical appearance is important in making impressions it matters very little if we are empty inside. This teaches us that some of the most valuable people God created may not look like we think they should look but indeed they may carry great weight in our destiny.

On occasion there have been rather perceptive girls who choose the tattered box near the end of the game. Most often it is not chosen but remains rejected by all of the workshop attendees. So, it is left for the last girl to take away. She has no other choice. Despite, having no choice and being forced into taking what seemed the invaluable leftovers, she walks away with twenty dollars.

This in itself is also a lesson for the girls. When we see others with shiny, dazzling, gifts, we tend to admire those gifts and people. Wonderful! But we must not forget the value in the gifts we possess. Though we may look at our gifts as tattered or common, there is great value inside of those gifts - great value that gives us the ability to walk away a little richer.

We should stop lying to each other and ourselves saying that our physical appearance does not matter. Our physical appearance usually makes the first impression. Self-care of our appearance is an appreciation for the shell God has given us. We cannot neglect or mistreat our physical appearance. Physical appearance matters.

However, physical appearance is not a very serious matter at all. The way we look is not the most significant issue in our lives, unless, of course, displeasure with your physical appearance begins to erode your mental and emotional esteem. In that case, you need to put some time into finding physical traits you love about yourself. Whether you find them inside of you, at the gym, or at a local hair salon, find a way to love the way you look.

So encourage yourself, your sons and daughters, nieces and nephews, sisters and brothers, mothers and fathers, aunts, uncles and friends to love and appreciate the way they look. Make it a point to say something affirming like, "You look amazing in that suit." Force them to accept the beauty that radiates from inside of them.

The more you plants seeds of self-esteem in others, the bigger your own esteem grows. It is a win-win and strikes a mighty blow to self-hatred and insecurity.

My favorite thing about my physical appearance is...

My Smile, my looks

-3-

"If you judge a fish by its ability to climb a tree it will live its whole life believing that it is stupid."
–Albert Einstein

The problem with going through intensive

exercises to identify our strengths and weaknesses is

that independently there is no such thing. Strength is

only a strength in a particular situation. Such is the

same with weakness. An ability to speak loudly is great

for being a cheerleader, not so much for being a

librarian. Therefore, talking loud is neither a strength nor a weakness. It is merely a trait we possess.

This paradigm shift in your thinking is foundational to building self-love and a true understanding of your identity. Our lane to purpose is not about what we have or do not have. It is about using what we have to the advantage of our purpose. Essentially, you need to find out what you have that works and work it.

If you do not feel like you have any talent or skill then you are looking at it all wrong. You are filled with characteristics and traits. It is your responsibility to find the best way to use those traits in order for them to be considered a strength. Einstein's fish could swim very well but that was not much help in trying to climb a tree.

Take an inventory of everything you can do. Jot down ten things that you can do. Do not give any thought to how good you are at them. Just write them down. After you write them down then put a star beside the things on the list you think you are particularly good at doing. Then go back and put a star by the things you really like to do. Does anything jump out with two stars?

Things I can do

1. _____

2. _____

3. _____

4. _____

5. _____

6. _____

7. _____

8. _____

9. _____

10. _____

Now, for the starred options on the list, identify a situation that would allow you to use that trait as a strength. For example, if you have "riding a bike" listed as something you can do you may want to list teaching children to ride bikes as a way to exhibit this as a strength. You could work with non-profit organizations to create bike-riding campaigns as fundraisers. You could join a circus and ride the bike around the center ring as a clown.

Do not limit your thinking. You may have giggled about the circus clown idea above but there are people who live very satisfied and fulfilled lives as circus clowns. They are gifted to give people joy. They make people laugh and the ability to ride a bike is a strength in that job. If you cannot ride a bike then you

cannot get the job riding around the center ring.

Situations Where My Traits Are Strengths

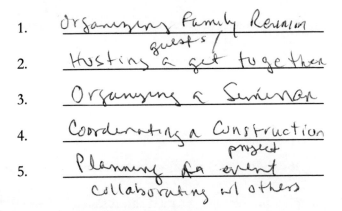

1. Organizing Family Reunion
2. Hosting a get to gether guests
3. Organizing a Seminar
4. Coordinating a Construction project
5. Planning an event
   Collaborating w/ others

When I first realized that I could write, my

mind immediately went to writing books. Then I

decided that I could write articles. I write articles about

motherhood because I am a mom. I got a dog so I started writing articles on dogs. I write newsletters, sales materials, presentations, etc. I can write and I love to write anything that has words.

Somewhere inside of you is a double-starred trait that you are both really good at and really enjoy. Maybe it did not immediately pop up in that first list of ten traits and abilities. But keep going. Keep listing things you can do. Match those to the right situation and Voila! You have strength. Using that trait will allow you to thrive and move toward identifying the purpose of your life. It will help navigate your lane.

When you receive feedback about a trait, you have a responsibility to discover whether that trait is truly a detriment to your purpose or if you are merely using it in the wrong situation.

You cannot allow comments and thoughts about your strengths and weaknesses to affect your self-esteem. Think about that poor fish that went through life believing he was stupid. Can you imagine it? Every day watching the cat run up the tree, feeling beaten, lowly and useless. Then one day someone takes the fish and the cat and throws them into the river. Suddenly, the fish is the stronger one, the smarter one, and the one with all the answers. The fish had not become a different animal. Neither did the cat. But they were put in a different situation and suddenly the perspective on the greatness of each animal changes.

When you are misaligned to a situation that does not play well to your traits, it may take time to course correct. That is okay. While you are in that misplaced situation you must constantly remind yourself that you are who you are regardless of your current situation. Do not confuse the assessment of your skills in that situation with a personal assessment of who you are. You are perfectly made for your lane. You just need to find it.

Finding your lane is an intersection of what you are really good at and what you really love. We'll keep reminding ourselves of this each day until we land in our lane. Just because you are really good at something does not mean it is what you want to do. If you do not want to do it, you probably were not meant to do it.

Over the span of your life you will find yourself in many situations. Some will play well to your traits and others will not. Once you realize that you are who you are for all of God's glory, you will be able to maintain your self-esteem despite the circumstance in your life.

I think I am at my best when...

I am connecting with people.

-4-

**"Opportunity is missed by some people because
it's dressed in overalls and looks like hard work"
– Thomas Edison**

We can look at other people and easily see that

they have advantages that we do not. We say, "No

wonder you scored. You started your life on third

base." Unlike track and field, we are all not given the

same start out of the blocks.

The child of well-known actors has a much

easier road to becoming an actor than the child of a

teacher. While the teacher's child is pounding out drama courses at the local community college hoping to land a paid gig, the actor's child is starring in a lead motion picture role. This is a reality and not one to be ignored if you are going to find your lane.

In order to seize your opportunities to be great there is one thing to remember: Everyone has an opportunity. Notice that I did not say that everyone has an equal opportunity. As people living in the United States of America we have opportunity to do absolutely anything we set our minds to doing. But therein lies the problem.

America has always been deemed the land of equal opportunity. Not true. We are all born with different genetic traits, raised in different environments and given exposure to different kinds of experiences. Barack Obama seized his opportunity to be President of the United States, but George Bush, whose father was also President, had a much easier opportunity. He was a born a white male in a patriarchy of Caucasian power majority. Not only was he born with this intrinsic opportunity, but he also knew someone who had been President and that someone happened to be his father. The latter two principles are extremely important to the development of a greatness mindset.

As children our minds are developed by the exposures we have. Good parents tell their children "you can be anything". However, that "anything" is defined only by those things that exist in the mind and exposures of the parent and the mind of the child. You cannot aspire be something that you have know no idea exists.

When we are searching for our purpose it is important to explore as many of our traits as possible. You never know what is hidden inside of you until you spend time looking around in there. Once you know what is inside then it is time to seize an opportunity. Remember that it will not be equal to someone else's opportunity. It might be tougher for you than the next person. But, you have your opportunity, nonetheless.

We are not often prepared for the hardship that comes with opportunity. Your belief in equal opportunity can be the biggest hurdle in your way. Opportunity is a "what" in your life. It is "what" you can accomplish. It is not "how" you will accomplish it.

The "how" for each of us is unique to our individual stories.

Sure, there are some basic premises to achievement. In order to be a lawyer you must graduate from law school. However, some people will work their way through law school while others have parents who pay the bill without stress. Some will be forced to balance family responsibilities while others will have no responsibility outside of themselves. Some students will have parents who are attorneys to consult with, while others will be the first in their families to ever attend college. On the first day of law school each student has an opportunity to graduate. Each does not have an equal opportunity to graduate.

The way you achieve your goals in comparison to someone else will be different and not equal. Do not develop perspective about how you will achieve your goals based upon the next person's journey. There are short straight lanes to achievement and longer winding lanes. Some lanes are smoothly paved with asphalt. Other lanes may be gravel or cobblestone. Some may even be made of broken glass. No matter the construction of your lane, stay focused on the opportunity ahead of you. Once you find the lane with your name on it, stay in your lane.

When we see someone who has it worse than we do we tend to appreciate our circumstance more. "It could always be worse," we say. On the other hand, when we see someone with an easier way to go than we do, we tend to make excuses for why we have not achieved what we set out to achieve in our lives. The accomplishment of another person has no bearing on what you will accomplish.

Figure out who you are, what traits you possess, and line those up with the best scenario to make it work for you. It does not matter if someone else had an easier or harder way to achieve the same goals. Stay focused on finding your purpose and heading out on a journey to fulfillment in life. Do what you love and what you are very good at doing. Stay in your lane.

Right now I have an opportunity to…

Help
make a person's financial
life Better.

But I am afraid of or afraid to…

If I am on the
Best Path to my Potential
Success

-5-

**"Being defeated is often a temporary condition.
Giving up is what makes it permanent."
-Maryilyn Vos Savant**

When faced with an opportunity that is laced

with obstacles, you have to look at those obstacles as

additional independent opportunities to make you the

best you can be. This will ultimately get you to your

finish line.

Everyone has obstacles. Some people have

fewer than others. Some people have larger ones. It

sounds cliché but the definite way to overcome your obstacles is to keep trying to find ways to overcome them. Go around them. Go through them. Go under them or over them.

People who have lost their legs can run in the Olympics if they keep pushing. When it comes to achievement, the more we overcome on our way to greatness the more we are able to overcome. Losing both legs makes it difficult to walk, a normal daily activity. With tenacity and endurance, you can go from walking to then running. After a while you learn to run faster and over time you could find yourself running in the Olympics. This is not simply a physical achievement. It is a mental, emotional and spiritual achievement as well.

Winning is a holistic experience. Everybody needs to win so they can feel what it is like to win. You learn from a winning experience. You learn to recognize what it feels like in your mind, body and soul to win. Your first "A" or your first job can light a fire of success beneath you. The first time you win an art contest can give you a bit of hope that you can be a successful artist.

I was so nervous when I wrote my first book, "Par for the Curse." It was my first novel. I was a rookie writer who had no formal writing education outside of my college English courses. I basically just had a story I wanted to tell. When I finished "Par for the Curse" it was a way for me to test the literary waters. Writing was something I loved, but I was not sure if I was any good at it.

As it turns out, "Par for the Curse" won an award at the New York Book Festival and was considered for an NAACP image award in Literature. It sparked a desire in me to continue to write. Now, I've written four books. That first small win created a momentum in me that propelled me forward along my journey.

Everybody needs a win. Everybody has a win. The problem is that we do not see our victories because we choose to look through external eyes rather than from inside of us. That addiction to comparison can beat away your esteem and ultimately cause you to give up on your goals.

In 2009, "Par for the Curse" was published by print on demand channels. It has sold over 5000 copies to date. That is ten times what the average first time author sells and far more than I expected to sell as an unknown writer. I am still so pleased with the performance of my first novel.

Two years later E.L. James wrote her first Print On Demand book. It was a book titled "50 Shades of Grey." She has sold over 100 million copies as a new writer. That is a 200,000 times what the average first time author sells.

Ms. James' accomplishment with Fifty Shades did not at all make me feel any less about my achievement with "Par for the Curse." I did not suddenly frown upon my 5000 copies. I had a goal and

I felt very good about achieving my goals. In fact, I more than surpassed my goals. Staying focused on my individual goals and achievements provided me with a "win" from which to build.

One day I may sell 100 million copies of a book. Maybe it will even be this one. But if it is not this one, I will not kick rocks and stop writing. Like you, I will achieve everything I want to accomplish if I just stay in my lane.

On the way to your greatness you will bump your head, skin your knees and run out of steam. That is quite okay. Take a minute, gather your thoughts and redesign your plan if you need to do so. Then, get back on it and use what you learned from the last obstacle to overcome the next one.

Successful people who can sustain their success have many things in common. One of those many things is the ability to endure and push beyond failures and setbacks. You have heard it said over and over again. We need to learn from our mistakes. Well, I say take it a step further. Learn from the mistakes of others.

Make connections with other purposeful people in your life. If you do not have any, get some now. On your journey to purpose, it is critical to find people who are already in their lane. They may be sprinting, jogging, walking, or even crawling but finding someone who has achieved their goals on purpose is crucial to developing a mental and emotional fitness toward winning.

I may need to catch my breath at times but I won't stop doing what I need to do to….

_____

A good example of someone in my life who knows how to succeed is ___*Judith Like*___ .

I am going to set up time to talk with him/her by the end of day on ___*(Done)*___ . *Stays in touch*

-6-

**"Find out who you are and do it on purpose."
– Dolly Parton**

Realizing that you do something really well is not the same as finding your "gift." Remember, a strength is simply a skill you have matched to the right situation. Everything you can do could be considered a strength in the correctly aligned environment.

You are able to do a lot of things and you are very good at some of those things. You can identify many situations where those things would be considered strengths and talents. These strengths and abilities will undoubtedly help serve your purpose during life's journey. However, there is a great difference between what you can do and what you were created to do. You were specifically equipped with certain traits to help you do what it is you were born to do. These gifts help you live out your purpose.

If you are a customer service person, you undoubtedly have a lot of skills. However, your purpose is not to work at the phone company. That is your job. It is the provision for you to maintain your life's needs.

Your purpose is deeper than that. Your purpose may be to show kindness and support to other people.

You could be gifted at putting people at ease. That could be in the form of a joyful greeting or a pleasant ear that does not react to their frustration.

When looking at the skills that you consider gifts go deeply into why you were given that gift and you will unveil your purpose. In work or play, in small things and large ones, that purpose should spring out of you. You may exercise your purpose at your job, but your job is not your purpose.

Being a pastor is a job. Leading people to Christ is a purpose. You do not need to be a pastor to lead people to Christ. You can accomplish this in many career choices. Doctors, teachers, and professional athletes can all lead people to Christ. However, if being a pastor is your job it aligns very well with your purpose of leading people to Christ. Get it?

My purpose is not to be a writer or a professional coach. However, both writing and coaching align with my purpose to infuse the world with love and self-esteem. Creating The Kamryn Adams Group was a vehicle to keep me in my lane. Across the groups operating companies, we produce traditional and online media content, publish books, offer personal coaching and business consulting. No matter which part of the business I am working on at the moment, my purpose of instilling other people with love is being fulfilled.

The ability to listen and make people feel good about themselves is a gift. Someone with this gift could be a hairdresser, a barber, a make-up artist, a motivational speaker, a day spa owner or a guidance counselor. Your gifts and purpose are WHO YOU ARE, not what you do.

If you do not know your gift, have no worries. The good news is that you were born with all of the gifts that you need during your lifetime. They are all wrapped up inside of you and life will pull out of you how you will use them. Your decision is to use them in the most fruitful and productive way possible.

Have you ever noticed that drug dealers are often excellent financial managers? They know how to make money from money. They understand financial principles and the economics of supply and demand.

They can go to prison and come out to huge life savings that they then turn into something productive.

There are charismatic leaders whom people naturally follow. These people were born with these leadership abilities that they chose to use in a variety of ways. Some of them become pastors and motivational speakers; others become pimps and street hustlers. You have two decisions to make on this journey. What are your gifts? Will you use them to live a fulfilling life of purpose or will you use them in a destructive manner?

Life becomes much easier when you realize that you have a unique mix of talents that are designed for you and only you. There comes a time in adulthood when you need to be okay with what you got and what you did not get. It would be an absurd waste of time for me to start taking singing lessons so I can sing for a living. Granted, singing for a living could be a way to live out my purpose of instilling self-love to others. But singing is not an ability or talent that has been given to me. It has been given to Christina Aguilera who sings "You are beautiful no matter what they say. Words can't bring you down....oh no. You are beautiful in every single way. Yes, words can't bring you down..." She inspires people with her singing. I hope to inspire you with my writing and speaking. It would be senseless for me to dwell on what I cannot do and miss the very gift that will allow me to live out my purpose.

Part of the frustration many people experience is that they are trying to develop gifts that have not been given to them. They see the way other people live or work and want those same traits and talents for themselves. This frustration is the beginning of self-hate. The more you try to accomplish something that you were not designed to do, the more inadequate you feel. Hence, the Einstein quote previously mentioned at the beginning of chapter two.

Einstein's perspective was that everybody is a genius when they find their niche. Finding your gifts and living out your purpose is a very important part of your esteem. You have to find out what you have that works and work it!

Suddenly you become the fish successfully swimming in water with grace that makes you feel alive. You will wonder why you ever tried to climb that darn tree. How silly would it be for a fish to feel bad because it cannot climb a tree?

It is equally as silly for you to think lower of yourself because of something you cannot do. If you were meant to do it, you would have the ability to do it. Do not base your self-esteem on the things you are unable to do. Instead, build an image of yourself based on all the things, big and small, that you CAN DO.

When is the last time you felt inadequate because you cannot fly like a bird? The answer is probably (and hopefully) never. You know that humans cannot fly. Therefore, you are good with not being able to fly. You know you were not created to fly so there is no pressure to soar through the air like a falcon. But, if by chance, some man figures out how to fly by flapping his arms and legs… there will be many people who suddenly feel like a flying failure. Though you never give any thought to flying because you realize it is not something you can do, the minute you see someone fly you begin to feel less talented, less skilled, less accomplished than the man who can fly.

It may sound silly and you may be saying to yourself that you would never be so ridiculous as to behave that way. However, it is that very behavior that we exhibit when we look at what someone else can do and feel bad about who we are. Staying in your lane means focusing on what you do well and accepting those things you cannot do. You live your life on purpose with what you have been given. Then you find true happiness and joy every day of your life.

So how in the world do you figure out what you are supposed to be doing? Take some time to examine what you really want to do. What is the thing that you believe you would do for free if only someone would give you chance? What do you dream about when you are sitting at work? That is the very thing you need to pursue to help live out your purpose.

Your purpose sits at the intersection of what you are really good at and what you love to do. That's why when we see people who are living in their purpose it looks effortless. Think Beyonce Knowles-Carter. Is there any doubt that she was put here to entertain us, to give us a few hours of joy? She could have done this in a number of ways. She has tried to entertain us with her acting but she is not that great at it. She's okay and she is certainly able to hold her own on screen. But she is not the effortless, mesmerizing, dynamic woman she is on stage. There is a difference in what you CAN do and what you were MADE TO DO.

Think about the time you felt the very best about yourself. Maybe it was in your dreams. Maybe it was a far off thought or an actual moment in your life. That is precisely what you should be doing. Then take a deeper look at that thing. How might you use it? What jobs or positions will allow you to optimize that thing you do. Discover your purpose. Make it work for you.

But wait! Hold on just a minute. This revelation of gifts and purpose does not mean that you go into your job tomorrow and announce to your boss and peers that you quit because you are on your way to

When people said they had a great time.

Family reunion

Bringing people together

Summer Reunion, etc.

destiny. That is certainly a great fantasy and you should meditate on the day when you can move further into your purpose. Until that time comes, continue to develop your gifts and be prayerful about how to use them to live on purpose.

Remember, your purpose is who you are. It exudes from you. It is an "I am…" not an "I do…" In some way on your current job – no matter what it is, your purpose should manifest.

During my time in the corporate world, I mentored and counseled numerous people in water cooler discussions and closed door sessions. I used my gift to live out my purpose in the environment of my provision.

My purpose is to bring people together.

Did you catch that? Repeat it to yourself. Write it on the wall. No matter where you are, your gifts and purpose will work for you from within. Some work environments may have a greater impact from your purpose than others. This is why we align our gifts and live life ON PURPOSE...to have the greatest impact on the world around us.

Sometimes working in our purpose is not our provision. The Apostle Paul was a tent maker. That was hardly his purpose but it was the provision that God sent to him in order for him to joyfully fulfill his purpose of spreading the gospel of Jesus.

Respect your ability to make an honest living and meet your living needs. At the same time, work with joy so that your gifts and talents help you even in a work environment that may not be directly aligned to your purpose.

There is nothing more disheartening than jumping out there "in faith" and then being forced to go backward because you did not wait on God's timing or plan for you. This can eat away at your self-esteem. It can instill fear and cause you to stop exploring who you are and what you have that works. Do not jump into the passing lane before you have enough acceleration to keep moving. It is frustrating and non-productive for everyone involved – you and those who work with you.

As you get more frustrated, then you may find yourself angry and resentful toward people who are living their purpose. Suddenly, you are so far out of

being who you were created to be that you are
miserable and do not know how to get back into your
lane.

It took many years for your self-esteem and
passion for life to erode. Be mindful that self-love, self-

awareness and living on purpose are a process. These
things take time to build just as they took time to
disappear.

You know, God is pretty big on process. I
know we want to think He just snaps his majestic
fingers and poof, "let there be…" Remember that
creating the whole world did not happen in that way.
The foundation of the world came in a snap, but the
whole world took seven days to create. That's process.

-7-

"Colors seen by candlelight will not look the same
by day."
– Elizabeth Barrett Browning

The more time you spend thinking about who

you are, the more your self-image will change. Looking

at yourself through a lens of love can show you a world

of possibility. They say if you change your mind you

can change your life. I believe this to be true.

Focus on the things that you do well and tie your esteem to those things. Do not be the fish that wants to climb the tree. Sure, you want to continue to work on building skills in other areas but at some point, after a reasonable attempt, you must realize that some skills and talents are just not in your lane.

During your journey to purpose, you need to make peace with your struggles and embrace your mistakes. Once you achieve the great and most difficult task of loving yourself, you will embrace who you have been created to be. This acceptance builds love inside of you. Then, and only then are you ready to blaze your personal trail with great success.

The key to staying in your lane is to remember that life is not a race for you to run against other people. It is a journey for you and you alone to fulfill a purpose that you are here to accomplish. You must stay focused on embracing your unique talents and skills to achieve purpose in your life. When you live your life on purpose you are miraculously filled with joy.

Do not be discouraged by the obstacles in front of you. They may be greater or fewer in number than someone who stands beside you. Avoid the temptation of comparison and simply keep your eyes focused on the journey ahead of you.

It will not be easy or without struggle, but the reward will be greater than the sacrifice. Anything worth having takes work. There is not greater work that self-development. It is a life-long process. As the author of this book I still enter times of self-exploration so that I continue to evolve into the perfectly purposed person that God created me to be.

Along the way, take time to celebrate that you are living in all of your greatness. You may have to remind yourself that it is okay to love who you are as long as you love and appreciate the greatness in those around you. Remember that your love for YOU should not diminish your love for others. You should not need to squash the esteem of others in order to love yourself. In fact, self-love is proportional. The more you learn to love who you are, the more you will love and exhibit that love to those around you. As you fill your heart with purposeful self-love it will push out things that oppose love like gossip, meanness, hatred and disloyalty toward others.

Celebrate the small victories in your self-love journey along the way. Celebrate when you take an opportunity to build someone up instead of tearing her down. Congratulate yourself when you realize that you have handled something differently than you would have before you started this journey.

Self-love and living on purpose go hand in hand. Until you know yourself and love yourself, you will never be able to live a life of purpose. Many people are miserable because they are living outside of their purpose. They feel like if they could change their life, they would feel better about themselves. In fact, the opposite is true. Love yourself and your life will change. Start the journey to self-love and find joy in living your life on purpose.

Your life does not get better or worse based upon the person in the lane next to you. You were born to the parents you were meant to have in the environment you were meant to experience. You were born with the skills and abilities that you were meant to have. Work those skills. Nurture those abilities. Do not be the fish trying to climb a tree. Find your water. Swim fast and free to your purpose and remember to STAY IN YOUR LANE.

-8-

EXERCISES and AFFIRMATIONS

**"Advice is what we ask for when we already know
the answer but wish we didn't."
– Erica Jong**

Let us start your exploration of self. This may

be a refresher or it may be brand new to you. It does

not matter where you are on the discovery spectrum

take some time to think about you. Clear your mind of

everyone else. Clear your mind of what people say you

can do and who they say you are. Dig deep within, in

quietness as you complete the exercise on the following pages.

Relax your body. Take a deep breath and close your eyes. Think about all of the words that just entered your spirit while you were reading this book. Sit in silence for as long as you need to then answer the following questions.

After reading this book I feel...

_____

_____

After reading this book I think...

_____

_____

After reading this book I am...

_____

_____

Things I like about myself…

1._____

2._____

3._____

4._____

5._____

I want you to repeat the things on this page every time you brush your teeth. You can say it out loud or in your mind but I want you to revisit this list daily, multiple times a day. "I like…."

Things I can do really well…

1. _____

2. _____

3. _____

4. _____

5. _____

Things I really love to do…

1. _____

2. _____

3. _____

4. _____

5. _____

Is there something that appears on both lists that excites you? Maybe all five things are the same on both lists. Conversely, if nothing matches then I suggest that you spend some more time in self-discovery and reflection.

Relax your mind again. Make your mind a blank slate. Visualize it as a wall of whatever color you chose. You can only see that color in front of you. Now say this statement out loud and let your heart speak the answer without thinking.

What I really want to do is…

_____

_____

_____

Repeat this goal in the affirmative before falling asleep at night. Before I wrote my first book I used to say this affirmation, "I will be an author." After a while, it became a positive confession, "I am an author." Before long my confession came to life and today I am an author of four books.

It is time to plan. How will you achieve the goal mentioned above? Answer the following:

I would be very good at this because….

1. _____

2. _____

3. _____

Now that we have uncovered what you want to do.
What are some of the obstacles you might face?
Though, there could be many along the way, let's take it
one step at a time.

Two obstacles in my way might be...

1. _____

2. _____

How will I get passed these obstacles?

_____

_____

_____

_____

If you completed the exercises on the previous pages you now have a plan to find your purpose. Meditate on this plan. Visualize yourself in its success. Work the plan. Stay focused on those things that will get you to your goal. Do those things that get your to purpose. Do not be the fish trying to climb a tree. STAY IN YOUR LANE!

Connect with Kamryn Adams on Social media
Facebook.com/kamrynadams
Twitter.com/kamrynadams
Instragram.com/kamrynadams
Pintrest.com/kamrynpins
Kamrynadams.blogspot.com

Email: Kamryn @KamrynAdams.com

To receive personal coaching from Kamryn

http://myalliancelife.com